QUIET CRACKS

ABHIPSA PATI

This book is dedicated to all the readers "who look up at the stars and wish".

Contents

Contents

Acknowledgements

Writing a book is harder than I thought and more rewarding than I could have ever imagined. None of this would have been possible without the constant support of my family.

So yet again if anyone from the family's reading it, here's my second book which I published as a surprise for you guys.

1. A Run

I run all the time
not well or fast
but my legs carry me
far enough
so as to think i've done something worthwhile
I like to run late in the afternoon
before darkness
and the exhaustion of the day spent
sets in
sometimes I look over my shoulder
as though I'm playing out a movie
and someone is following me
no one ever is though
and I smile to myself
in surreal relief
because that doesn't happen
in the real world
to people like me
except it does
in the real world
to people like me

2. Numb

We light candles and say prayers for those who have gone.
Our thoughts and feelings keep them alive in our hearts forever
And in the night when we can't sleep that's when we remember.
Even though they are gone from this world
We can not let them be
We hold on to the most precious thing we have
And that's our memory.
I hope that memory serves you well I hope that you'll be alright
I hope that you are touched by god's hand and blessed with all his might.
Life is hard to live without them each and every day
And for all people's good intentions
There is nothing you can really say.
We wish that we could speak to them to tell them how much we miss them.
And we wish that they could talk back so that in turn we could listen.
A numbness creeps inside of us.
It's hard to get to go away.
Forever in our heads and hearts is where they will always stay,
If you've lost someone dear to you and you feel like the sadness won't end.
Know that I am here for you if ever you need a friend.

3. Of the Willow Tree

She pondered her escape
And to the woods she fled
Only the coat on her back
And a pillow for her head
She pictured the old tree
As a child she would climb
And hopelessly wondered
Could she find room inside
Would its mossy branches
Hold her as they once did
Would its leaves give shelter
And keep her secret well hid
Tired of the modern world
Grown bored with society
She was now and forever
A woman of the willow tree

4. Reminscing

As I gazed up at the vast cosmos,
I end up focusing on a single solitary star.
It shone brighter than the others.
I wished for it to take me back, but not too far.
I'd go back in a heartbeat if only I could choose
To a time when I thought that I could never lose.
To those moments of laughter, when all was well and good.
To the time I spent with friends every second that! could.
Now life has gotten busy and it's hard to make the time.
Gone are the days I took for granted in my prime.
So I've wished upon this star, already knowing it won't come true,
But still, I'm thankful for all the good times that was able to share with you.

5. Quiet Cracks

I wanted to scream
as loud as my lungs would allow
but I had to whimper and squeak
like an injured mouse
if my heart had to break
it had to do so quietly
behind closed doors
so they couldn't hear
the shards of pain
crack the kitchen floor
they talk of sleepless nights
and ceaseless worry
self doubt and tired eyes
but what of the brave faces
and painted smiles
these cannot be measured
in hours of rest
clawed back with a nap
they live in the lines of our faces
secrets forever lost in cracks

6. Lie

Hoping that we won't be discovered, we hide,
We might fake a smile, but are broken inside,
Of us, there's a side
That needs a guide
A person with whom we can confide
So we don't have to hide our true side
When we say we are fine,
We lie

7. The debt must be paid

We all owe a debt from the moment we are born.
The only time we really think about it is when we feel forlorn.
It's not easy to think about it day after day
The longer we think, the further from ambition we stray.
Death in itself is nothing to fear.
It's what we leave behind that keeps us here.
Don't get me wrong, my feelings are strong and I have plenty of lasting regrets
But life is for the living, so it's good to be forgiving.
After all we must pay our debts.
I'm in no hurry for them to bury me, it's not what I want one bit,
But if this life should choose that I should lose then I'll gladly take the hit.
What awaits beyond our fates, is it heaven or hell?
People weep as we go six feet deep, and leave our mortal shell.

8. Anxiety doesn't knock first

I lied and said I was busy.
I was busy;
but not in a way most people understand.
I was busy taking deeper breaths.
I was busy silencing irrational thoughts.
I was busy calming a racing heart.
I was busy telling myself I am okay.
Sometimes, this is my busy -
and I will not apologize for it.

9. Lost Property

It's not in my coat my pocket
I'll check my jeans
it's maybe on a cold wash
in the washing machine
or was it in the cupboard
beneath the stairs
buried in all the random crap
that lives under there
it could be in the drawer
the one with all the leads
sometimes I shove stuff there
I might one day need
ah I cant quite recall
when I last had it
Tl check if mum knows
maybe it got thrown in the attic
nowhere to be seen
I'm at a loss to where it could be
if anyone finds it
please return my inner peace

10. Mirrors

I was only eighteen years old when it happened to me
Ever since that day, my face I can no longer see
I can't look in a mirror, I can't even look at a pane of glass
Lest I see my reflection whenever I may pass.
It's hard to explain what I'm trying to convey
My whole damn life has been thrown into disaray.
I know it sounds mad but it follows me room to room
This thing that follows me only trying to consume.
It's made life difficult but somehow I'm still alive
I never could have imagined so long of this I would survive.
I hear it in my sleep, it often talks to me
Trying to convince me that I'm all I'll see.
I only ever saw it once and that was enough of a warning.
I saw my own body sort of shifting and transforming
It was no longer me and I could feel it in my chest
Luckily for me that once I was suddenly blessed.
The mirror fell off the wall and landed on its face
I felt it leaving my body without even the faintest trace.
Ever since that day, I've never looked directly at my own reflection.

Staying away from mirrors is now my only protection.

11. Therapy

Don't listen to the nay sayers,
Therapy can work a treat.
It will help you with everyday situations
And also with people you meet.
If you feel as though something isn't right,
No one knows your mind better than you.
If you need to talk to someone,
Then that's what you definitely should do.
Maybe you feel you aren't ready? Or that
"therapy's not for me".
Well, the sooner you get rid of those ideas
the better,
Because it can get harder to repair a
damaged psyche.
So if you feel in need, stop putting it off
Forget about those you think might scoff.
Keep that promise you made to yourself
And start to look after your mental health.

12. Message To Death

Hello death, how are you? It's
been quite a while,
Since our last chance encounter
when you acted quite hostile.
I nearly drowned far from my
home.
1 panicked what can I say?
i'm just rather grateful that you
spared me on that fateful day.
I wonder what it's like to walk a
mile in your shoes.
Taking people's friends and
family away probably often gives
you the blues.
1 know it can't be an easy job,
maybe you could take a holiday?
Go somewhere nice and warm?
You know what they say about
all work and no play.
Sometimes when I read the news
I think of you a lot.
And all the people you leave in
this world absolutely distraught.
1 know that there is a plan in

motion that you must obey,
But wouldn't it be nice if you
could just let our loved ones
stay?

13. Vincent

From his iron-barred window,
he sat swirling brushstrokes
of yellow and blue.
Round and round
he caressed the canvas
painting lucid dreams.
Bandaged on his left side
sounds were softened
though he could still
make out the screams.
Hands in tact
and lunacy only fleeting
he bled a Starry Night.
For it is always the broken
behind the masterpiece.

14. Uniquity

We may not be the same, but no one is superior.
That would have to mean that other people are inferior.
Everyone holds a different tool kit to use in this existence.
Some choose to go in hard, others take the path of least resistance.
Strengths and weaknesses are variable. To each their own.
Whatever it is you are good at, that's the skills you should hone.
We naturally enjoy things we are good at. It gives us a sense of pride.
Don't believe anyone is better than you. Don't let your own skills be denied.
Remember what you are good at, write it down on a list.
It might not be easy at first but don't let anything go by dismissed.
We all have our own special gifts. Things that mean a lot to us.
If people make you feel down about yours, then maybe they're not worth the fuss?

15. The Red Stone

Down in the forest, there's a place you can go.
It's a place you can be sure that not many men know.
There is a rock with a rather magical aura
You may find it hidden deep amongst the flora.
This rock is not like others, it's smooth, red and looks out of place.
Don't worry, you'll feel it's draw if you enter its space.
They say an ancient magic from days long past still lingers in the air around it.
Magic that was made to last. Only the lucky may find it.
The story goes that a wise druid had placed it there.
That he was magnificent, and had a real flair
But power corrupts, it is all consuming
Nothing could stop the hatred for others brewing
He became twisted and gnarled. Wanted to show off his might.
So he cast a spell so powerful and dark it turned day into night.
The locals were worried. The druid was out of control
They tried to talk to him, but there was no saving his soul.
Consumed by the darkness, he had once been so kind
Now corrupted by the stone he did find.
No longer affable, he'd become a real threat
He began waging a war on the locals, one they'd never forget.
He wanted everything and knew it was well within his power.
The locals worried that they were getting closer to their final hour.
They knew they didn't stand a chance to take him head on

So they set fire to the whole forest at what they thought was dawn.
From deep within the forest they heard the druid screaming out
Casting incantations, their head's were filled with doubt.
But then the fire reached the druid who had stayed by his precious stone.
When the forest fire died all that they found of him was bone.
Beware the stone. They say it can grant anything the heart desires
But be warned, there's a price: Your life it requires.

16. A Pensive Mood

Why do we do it?
Give into our selfish desire?
It cuts our souls deep,
Like fine cheese wire.
It doesn't make us happy
We then have to live with the regret
Aiming for higher status
From those we've barely met.
My question remains unanswered
But I've given it a lot of thought.
The more we aim for "happiness"
The less happy we are with what we've got.

17. Brown Storm

It has always been like this.
My mother and me waking up together,
Elbows touching in the morning-
her knee pain crack, my porous yawns that filled the air.
Her forehead sprouting in the firm sunlight
Tea of jasmine flower and ginger,
Quilts of firm solitude/ leafing into a permanent parentheses.
Her turmeric pickle hands hovering into oblivion.
Dawn- dusk-fingers intertwined.
Lips retrieving, a puddle, a womb of stars.
It has been this way where I could roam into her fuller arms/ horizons traveled/ hibiscus in the hair.
Nothing much yet is perfect.
Depths of the starry ocean. Static. Motion.
I told her many a time, that she needed rest. A leisure.
Hand-painted dupattas. I told her everything about politics, the universe, filthy neighbors. All of it.
She sews it all, somehow. Healed. Sun-kissed.

She-a string from birth to birth.
Hedge of winters. A shriek that could instigate a
process of rebirth.
A constant brown storm.

18. Warning

When I am an old woman I shall wear purple
With a red hat which doesn't go, and doesn't suit me.
And I shall spend my pension on brandy and summer gloves
And satin sandals, and say we've no money for butter.
I shall sit down on the pavement when I'm tired
And gobble up samples in shops and press alarm bells
And run my stick along the public railings
And make up for the sobriety of my youth.
I shall go out in my slippers in the rain
And pick flowers in other people's gardens
And learn to spit.
You can wear terrible shirts and grow more fat
And eat three pounds of sausages at a go
Or only bread and pickle for a week
And hoard pens and pencils and beermats and things in boxes.
But now we must have clothes that keep us dry
And pay our rent and not swear in the street
And set a good example for the children.
We must have friends to dinner and read the papers.
But maybe I ought to practise a little now?
So people who know me are not too shocked and surprised
When suddenly I am old, and start to wear purple.

19. I Love You

Baby, it's your trauma versus your wellness..
And it's only you who can fight it with all your willingness.
When some ONE rejects you..
Don't forget that there are so many more who adore you.
Your healing will come with hope..
Don't lose it.. no.. no..no... Nope!!
So breathe in and breathe out.
And give happiness a Shout Out!!
Every time when someone compares you..
Give yourself a rose and say "I love you".

20. Full

It was as full as it ought to be
as biology intended
the atria receiving
ventricles releasing

.

all that tissue surrounding
like bubble wrap around china
the endo
the myo
so on and so on

.

it was all very complicated
but as I understood it was full
and yet it seemed
there was always room for more

21. Mental mess

Minds are unraveling on the floor
like spools of multi-coloured yarn
in a bungling cat's paws.
I stand frozen in the middle, for
I am scared of cats, but also inept
at knitting unspooled threads
into a sensible sweater or sock,
even though in my guilty hands I hold
two good needles and a tightly wound
ball of perfectly good yarn.
I stick the ends of my needles neatly
into the wool, the other ends
into my eyes; I cannot bear
to see any longer the pain around me
while I stay completely warm

22. Hours

It's strange
It's weird
It's frustrating
It's a never ending stream of thoughts
How did I never notice before
Why can't I stop overthinking
When will I get my answers
Procrastination
Sensitivity
Impatience
It's all starting to make so much sense
I am allowing myself kindness
It's okay to notice my patterns
There is so much to devour
Though, there are simply not enough hours!

23. To the infinity

Locked in my body
I had a story
A story nobody ever knew
A story that made me blue.
Nobody knows about me
Just knows what I wanna be.
I know how much I felt lost
I know it was not that just all.
A new land
All alone
No memory
I couldn't go home
I struggled to find my way
All alone in a new place.
With unknown people all around
I just made my way
To a new place
A new memory
A New journey
To the infinity.

24. December rain

The tree is nourished
And inside I am warm
Drenched with understanding of what
I don't want
The rain and leaves
drip separation
Remind me of being re-born

25. Leap

Why are you here, at this hour, so late?
Why are you not on the pavement of faith?
You stand on the ledge, waterfalls on your face
You whisper words but I hear them too late
I dream of a forest with trinkets full
I see faces that were gone too soon
I know of bridges that have seen too much
I hear of woods with souls untouched
I don't want to hear of another one gone
I don't want to see another leap below
Please listen it's never too late
If you're to leap, then leap into my weight
I will hold you, hug you and cry.
Whispering to your ear, "Don't leave my side"
Who did this to you? Who pushed you this far?
Was it humans or the demons in your mind?
If you decide not to choose me, I will leap onto you.
You will struggle in my arms but I will hold on.
But should your body go limp in my limbs.
Then and only then will the fear seep in.
For you who is ready to see the other side,
For you and all the demons you try to hide
Please know it will be alright.
For every person who attempts to leap,

Know that there are people who will leap for you

26. You

The winds would stop blowing, there won't be any sunset...
If mom you are not in my day I would bet...
You are the destination to whom I would reach every day...
You are the one who first taught me to make a pot out of clay...
You are the heartbeat which would never be stopped...
You are the happiness who made all the sadness cropped...
Whatever you taught me about all the life is never gonna go away...
I want you as my mom even in all the coming lives, that's what I would say...
Sorry for the times i have lied or I have hurt you ever...
You know right I love you more than forever...
Having you as my companion, my friend, my everything is the great God's favor.
You wouldn't know how much blessed I am to have you as my mother...

27. Before me

Anxiety wakes up before me and waits.
When my alarm goes off it's there ready.
It plunges it's hands into my belly and
jiggles it's fingers but I don't feel it yet.
Tired, I stumble into the bathroom, urinate.
Then as I stand and pull up my nickers that's
when I feel it's fist churn in my stomach.
Hunched over the basin I stare down the
sink hole. I wonder if I'll throw up.
My heart feels like it's trying to squeeze out of
the gaps in my rib cage and tears slide down
my face. My body judders like an old car.
I am full on crying and I don't understand why.
I just want to go back to bed.
I never new I could be simultaneously so full of
adrenaline and exhaustion.
I feel my back straighten, my mouth fills with siliva,
gushes of perspiration flood my armpits and I retch.
I turned to face the toilet and watch bile hit the
water. I stare at my sick in a trance, wondering
what it would be like to wake up first, before
anxiety or better yet to wake up without it being
there at all.

28. Apologize

I thought I was showing anger,
not recognising that,
I was setting myself ablaze to the flames of anger,
I thought I was respecting myself,
not recognising that,
I was developing ego in that process,
I thought I was being cautious about future,
not recognising that,
I was over thinking about the things I have no control over,
I thought I was right all the time,
not recognising that,
I was manipulating others to agree with me,
I thought I was caring and protective,
not recognising that,
I was being over possessive about people crossing my limits,
May be its high time I should apologize for everything I did.

29. Knock Knock

"Wakey wakey! Good morning
sunshine!" "Come on girl, put on a big smile." The mirror
conversing with me every time,
As soon as the birds chirp with the picturesque sunrise.
I don't let any light in, not a single ray. "Come on, draw
open the curtains", the mirror says.
Not having this conversation again, not today,
All dressed up, lipstick on and there I go for my day.
Passing by people, all smiles.
After all, mirror told me, I can't deny
I pass my day, come home, looking satisfied.
I fooled the mirror but to myself, I can't lie.
The night follows up and I draw open the curtains,
But I make sure that I've locked the door, yeah, certain.
I curl up in my bed with the same apprehension,
And the silent wails in me start to build up tension.
I am scared that the melancholy monster would strike
again.
The mirror in front of me says, "face the pain." As soon as
the clock strikes one,
There he is at my door, loading bullets of my fears into a
gun.
I hear a bang at my door,
Scared, I look through the peephole. "There he is", I

exclaim to the mirror
My spine turning cold with a shiver. "Knock knock sweetheart, let me in.
I look at the mirror, "let him in". "Knock knock! Let me in." I shook my head but I hear, "let him in." "knock knock knock knock knock knock!"
NO! Leave me alone.
The mirror pushes me to the wall.
It says, "face your fears, they come for all." Shaking my head from left to right,
Not knowing what to do, my body being consumed by fright.
The knocking turns into pounding "Let me in!", he screams.
With my head in my arms, frowning I inch closer to the door as I shriek.
Finally, I open the door
He pushes me down,
Shoots me in the head
And now, I lay on the floor.
They say your fears leave when you face them
But my fears became the air that I breathe.
No, I don't have anxiety.
No, I don't have immense stress.
No, I'm not depressed.
I just need some help.
I ONLY NEED SOME HELP.

30. Untold

Let's take a walk on the road
Where everyone comes and everyone goes,
But people always say Hi, Hello to their mobile modes,
What's going on in life road is still untold.
During this walk, feelings are overflowed
Where everything is difficult to close,
But still, my heart manage to upload,
What's going on in life road is still untold.
What will happen in walk is secret code
Where we are finding our own flows,
But we will never know how to decode,
What's going in life road is still untold.
Everyone's life files are download
And they are happy as they don't know,
But download files will slowly show all the episodes,
What's going in life road is still untold.

31. Stories

When I see people on roads going on with their chores...
I don't see random traffic..
I see stories...
I see stories of people...
Carrying their responsibilities on shoulders
Trying to keep on with their lives somehow
I see people who have a family to feed
And also people who never have been cared
I see people that have something they're struggling with
But also have something that can make them laugh
And something that can bring them down to tears
Each have something they're dreaming of
Something they're looking forward to at their destination
And sometimes, something they're fearing to face when they reach
Somebody's arms to bury into, at home
Somebody that love them
Someone that they love
Someone they put their lives on
Someone they miss
And someone they're grieving upon
I see stories...
Stories of dreams and hopes,
Of anxiety and distress,
Of grief and loss,

Of love and passion
Stories... So similar to that of mine
Yet so uniquely entirely different.

32. Will I ?

I worried a lot. Will the garden grow, will the rivers
flow in the right direction, will the earth turn
as it was taught, and if not how shall
I correct it?
Was I right, was I wrong, will I be forgiven,
can I do better?
Will, I ever be able to sing, even the sparrows
can do it and I am, well,
hopeless.
Is my eyesight fading or am I just imagining it,
am I going to get rheumatism,
lockjaw, dementia?
Finally, I saw that worrying had come to nothing.
And gave it up. And took my old body
and went out into the morning,
and sang.

33. Some more

As summer passed by, I had always
missed my winter cries.
Those not-so-warm comforted nights.
Was all I had for my unfitted smiles.
Rolling under my sheets all night,
All I did was resting my eyes.
For they had cried for nothing but a few
anxieties of mine.
When I got them I was already struck,
Overthinking some unnecessary stuff.
Locked in and out often, for I never knew
how unreasoned was my every worth.
Scribbled out on some paper sheets,
Turning into some rhythmic tweets.
Made me relieved and in peace.
For all i wrote was heart poured.
And here I went and wrote some more.

34. Ending because of me

It's like the world is ending
And its ending because of me
The sky is falling
And its falling down on me
I'm scared of the dark
'Cause that's where I used to be
I'm scared of the silence
'Cause it's creeping up inside of me
All the he said, she said's giving me anxiety
Mother, you raised a good daughter
But they never see the good
No matter how tall I stand
I think I'm gonna fall
Tell me father, what do you do
When you do everything
But it's still not enough
Teach me how to get back up
When it all starts eating me up
When I keep bottling up my fears
Tell me how to survive the dark
When I can't stop my tears
Tell me how to not fall apart
It's like the world is ending
And it's ending because of me

35. Me

My mind is crossing by,
Lots of thoughts,
So, I thought to write.
But, as I put my fingers
On keyboard,
I suffered.
I can't write.
I can't put down the thoughts
Which are to and fro
Up and down
I'm looking at the ceiling
It's 2 o'clock
The night is here,
My Darkness
Crawled through my covers
Suddenly I'm scared,
I closed my eyes
Too tight,
I grabbed the covers
Hold them
Too tight
Then, there is the ray of something,
I can see,
What was that?

Dark blue rays
Blue rays of anxiety
Which hold me
through my throat
And tried to kill me down
My heart started
Pounding
I was sweating
Without knowing the way
How to cope?
I started saying
Those three words
That calms me
But then, suddenly something
Pushed me from my bed
And keep punching my face
I tried to see it
But it's invisible
It was sadness
I tried to save myself
And ordered my brain
To generate dopamine
But it was half asleep
It was 2 AM
So, I picked up my phone
With trembling hands
Saw his picture
That made me a Lil happy
The Darkness

Swept away
From my sheets,
The anxiety
Ran away with its feet,
The sadness
Went on his next new meet
As they all leave
I got calm
My heart gets normal
My breathing settles
That's how I make poems
When I don't want to write
But still want to write
That's how I deal with anxiety
I sent a long para to him
Telling him how much he means to me.
As when he would wake up
Tomorrow morning,
Only the pretty smile will be on his face,
And the reason
Would be me.

9 798888 056134

Printed by Libri Plureos GmbH in Hamburg,
Germany